This or That Pets

Is a SNAKE or a LIZARD the Pet for Me?

by Cara Krenn

PEBBLE
a capstone imprint

Published by Pebble, an imprint of Capstone
1710 Roe Crest Drive, North Mankato, Minnesota 56003
capstonepub.com

Copyright © 2025 by Capstone. All rights reserved. No part of this publication may be reproduced in whole or in part, or stored in a retrieval system, or transmitted in any form or by any means, electronic, mechanical, photocopying, recording, or otherwise, without written permission of the publisher.

Library of Congress Cataloging-in-Publication Data is available on the Library of Congress website.
ISBN: 9780756579197 (hardcover)
ISBN: 9780756579142 (paperback)
ISBN: 9780756579159 (ebook PDF)

Summary: Scaly bodies. Eye-catching spots and stripes. Snakes and lizards are fun, interesting pets! Compare these two reptiles side by side. Which is more active? Is one easier to clean up after than the other? Is one easier to bond with? Learn the answers to these questions and more. Then decide which one might make the best pet for you!

Image Credits
Capstone Studio: Karon Dubke, 6, 16; Shutterstock: A3pfamily, 15, davemhuntphotography, 9, Dirk M. de Boer, 10, Eric Isselee, 8, 20, Gary_Ellis_Photography, 11, GOLFX, 19, Helza Nitrisia, Cover (bottom), I Wayan Sumatika, 21, Krisda Ponchaipulltawee, Cover (top), Marina Veder, 7, Natasha Pankina, background (throughout), Nynke van Holten, 5, Phuwadon Phichairat, 17, Robert Eastman, 4, Sergey Novikov, 14, Siarhei Kasilau, 18, Steve Collender, 12, Yasemin G, 13

Editorial Credits
Editor: Carrie Sheely; Designer: Bobbie Nuytten; Media Researcher: Jo Miller; Production Specialist: Whitney Schaefer

Dedication: For Caroline and Kelly

Any additional websites and resources referenced in this book are not maintained, authorized, or sponsored by Capstone. All product and company names are trademarks™ or registered® trademarks of their respective holders.

Printed and bound in China. PO 5834

Table of Contents

Getting a New Pet 4
Equipment 6
Cheap or Costly 8
Rodent or Insect Meals 10
Clean or Messy 12
Social or Not 14
Watching Your Pet 16
Short or Long Lives 18
Which Pet Is Best for You? 20
    Glossary 22
    Read More 23
    Internet Sites 23
    Index 24
    About the Author 24

Words in **bold** are in the glossary.

Getting a New Pet

Tongues flick the air. Scaly bodies slither and crawl. Both snakes and lizards make great pets!

Snakes and lizards are **reptiles**. They have a lot in common. But they have differences too. See which pet might be better for you!

Equipment

Snakes and lizards need to live in escape-proof tanks. Many small snakes and lizards can live in 20-gallon tanks. Your pet may need a bigger tank as it grows. You can add branches and rocks to the tank. You need a tank liner for the bottom.

Snakes and lizards are **cold-blooded**. They cannot control their body heat. You need to buy heat lamps for them.

Cheap or Costly

Snakes can be more **expensive** to buy than lizards. But a pet's cost depends on the kind you choose. Lizards such as bearded dragons and leopard geckos are fairly cheap to buy. A Rankin's dragon can cost more than $300.

Snakes can be costlier over time. Snakes often live longer than lizards. Lizards tend to be cheaper to feed.

Rodent or Insect Meals

Snakes eat **rodents**. Owners warm up frozen mice for snakes to eat. If a dead mouse sounds yucky to you, it may be hard to feed a snake! You do not need to feed snakes every day. Most eat about once a week. Snakes eat their food whole.

Lizards mostly eat live insects. They eat crickets, mealworms, and cockroaches. They need to eat more often than snakes.

Clean or Messy

Which pet is messier? Snakes don't poop a lot. But lizards do! Owners clean up their poop every day.

Reptiles shed their skin as they grow. This is called **molting**. Snakes shed their outer layer of skin all at once. The old skin needs to be removed from the tank.

Social or Not

Snakes are not **social** pets. They do not make faces. They have no eyelids and do not blink. Some snakes can be held. Snakes like to live alone.

Lizards can be friendly. Some can be held gently. They may walk onto your hands. Some lizards can live together.

Watching Your Pet

You can watch snakes and lizards **bask** in the heat. They hide and rest in the shade. Snakes are often still. They are quiet. Many people find them calming to watch.

Lizards are usually more active than snakes. They can be **entertaining**. You can watch them wave their arms and bob their heads.

Short or Long Lives

A pet snake or lizard is a big **responsibility**. How long your pet lives depends on its type and care. Lizards can live around 15 years. Snakes can live more than 20 years.

Which Pet Is Best for You?

Think about what you know about snakes and lizards. What things are the same? What things are different? This activity might help you find out which one would be best for you!

What You Need:

- paper
- pencil or pen

What You Do:

1. Make a chart with two columns, one for snakes and one for lizards. Next to your columns, write down different categories. They can include feeding, clean-up, socialness, and fun to watch.

2. Think about each category. Mark an X in the column that matches what you would like more. For example, if you would rather feed a lizard, put an X in the lizards column.

3. When you are done, add the X marks in your snakes column. Then add the X marks in your lizards column. Which column has more? This could be the pet for you!

Glossary

cold-blooded (KOHLD-BLUHD-id)—having a body temperature that changes with the surrounding temperature

entertain (en-tur-TAYN)—to amuse and interest

expensive (ik-SPEN-siv)—very costly

molt (MOHLT)—to shed an outer layer of skin

reptile (REP-tile)—a cold-blooded animal that breathes air and has a backbone; most reptiles have scales

responsibility (ri-spon-suh-BIL-uh-tee)—a duty or a job

rodent (ROHD-uhnt)—a mammal with long front teeth used for gnawing; rats, mice, and squirrels are rodents

social (SOH-shuhl)—wanting to be near people or animals

Read More

Feldman, Thea. *Snakes Smell with Their Tongues!: And Other Amazing Facts.* New York: Simon Spotlight, 2021.

Hughes, Catherine D. *Little Kids First Big Book of Reptiles and Amphibians.* Washington, D.C.: National Geographic Partners, 2020.

Starkey, Michael G. *Reptiles for Kids: A Junior Scientist's Guide to Lizards, Amphibians, and Cold-Blooded Creatures.* Berkeley, CA: Rockridge Press, 2020.

Internet Sites

ChildFun: Fun & Interesting Lizard Facts for Kids
childfun.com/articles/general/interesting-lizard-facts-for-kids

National Geographic Kids: Reptiles
kids.nationalgeographic.com/animals/reptiles

Tampa Veterinary Hospital: Your First Pet Snake–the Best Choices
tampavet.com/exotics-blog/best-beginner-snakes

Index

activity levels, 16, 17

being held, 14, 15

cost, 8, 9

eating, 10, 11

heat lamps, 7

insects, 11

life spans, 18

molting, 13

pooping, 12

rodents, 10

socialness, 14, 15

tanks, 6, 13

About the Author

Cara Krenn writes children's books and for a variety of kids' magazines. The topics she writes about range from trash trucks to magical creatures. Cara loves the beach, dance music, and morning walks with her cowardly dog. She is a graduate of the University of Notre Dame and lives in sunny San Diego, California, with her husband, twin daughters, and son.